Courageous Advocacy and Political Neutrality in Schools

A Guide for Leaders and Governors

Richa

CW01619798

GROVE BOOKS LIMITED
RIDLEY HALL RD CAMBRIDGE CB3 9HU

Contents

Anglican Association of Directors of Education

The cover image is copyright © Grove Books Ltd

Copyright © Richard Hopkins 2023

First Impression October 2023
ISSN 2041-0964
ISBN 978 1 78827 347 3

1

Why Encourage Courageous Advocacy in Schools?

Do you remember the original *Star Trek* television series? If so, you will undoubtedly recall Captain Kirk's speech at the beginning of each episode: 'These are the voyages of the Starship Enterprise. Its five-year mission: to explore strange new worlds; to seek out new life and new civilizations; to boldly go where no man has gone before!'

I have the privilege of speaking regularly to groups of leaders and governors from Church of England schools about what it means to have a theologically-rooted Christian vision for their school. I sometimes start by showing them the famous *Star Trek* opening sequence in order to help them to understand the difference between a mission and a vision. For any organization, school or otherwise, a mission is what they want to achieve. Captain Kirk is clear about his mission, and schools are often clear about their mission too, whether it be their students' exam results, or the further education and employment destinations they want them to aspire to.

Ofsted's concept of the 'curriculum intent' is just such a mission. According to their inspection handbook, this is 'the knowledge and skills that pupils will gain at each stage through the school's curriculum.'[1] It is a mission because it asks *what* is being taught, not *why*. A school may, therefore, have a clear mission but no clear vision. That is because a school's vision is an explanation of why the school does what it does, both within and beyond the formally taught curriculum, in order to be clear about the kind of people it wants its students to become.

This book is about the concept of courageous advocacy. This can never just be part of a school's mission but must fully be part of its vision. It is about the sort of people the school wants to mould, rather than simply the knowledge they are taught. You can have a vision without courageous advocacy, but you cannot have courageous advocacy without a vision. In fact, the way that a school engages with courageous advocacy becomes, by default, the school's vision. And if the school is a Church of England school, then that courageous advocacy and its associated vision must grow out of Christian theological roots.

You cannot have courageous advocacy without a vision

The starting point for understanding how courageous advocacy works in detail is the May 2021 document *Courageous Advocacy*, written by Caroline Weir on behalf of Christian Aid and the Church of England Education Office.[2] At the heart of courageous advocacy are the three steps of *knowing, saying* and *doing*. Often summarized by the phrase 'beyond the bake sale,' the courageous advocacy process encourages pupils and adults to become agents for change by learning about issues of justice, as well as speaking out about them and taking action. This approach contrasts with the traditional charitable activity of raising and giving money to good causes. For a school embracing courageous advocacy, such an approach is not enough, however generous or compassionate it may be. The link with a school's vision is clear: does the school want to develop people who accept the inevitability of injustice while attempting to alleviate its symptoms, or does it want to encourage them to work actively to right the wrongs inherent in the injustice?

It is in taking the second and third steps of speaking out and actively working against injustice that a school can come up against its duty of political impartiality. Raising money for those who suffer injustice can be safe and comfortable. Relief can be provided without digging deep into the question of why the relief is needed. But if schools are to encourage students to speak out against injustice, the criticism of those responsible for the injustice moves from being implicit to explicit. As George Orwell wrote in his *All Art is Propaganda* critical essays, 'In our age there is no such thing as "keeping out of politics." All issues are political issues.'[3] If, therefore, schools engage their pupils with issues of justice, then they inevitably involve them in politics. Quite rightly, school leaders and governors are wary of doing this. A school's job is to educate, not indoctrinate. In addition, the parents, staff and governors in a school are likely to hold a wide range of opinions on key political issues. Leaders worry that, by engaging pupils with moral and political issues, they will inevitably alienate at least some members of their school community.

A school's job is to educate, not indoctrinate

Squaring the Circle

In this book, I want to offer practical advice for school leaders and governors about how to square this circle. I believe it can be done and done well. A successful vision unites an organization as everyone works towards a common goal. If courageous advocacy is the bedrock of vision, and vision is a uniting force, then courageous advocacy, if applied wisely, can be that force for the common good that all Church of England schools aspire to. A community is never going to be united by politics, but it can be united by the example of Christ and the desire to see everyone transformed to live 'life in all its fulness.'

In this book I will attempt to identify what successful courageous advocacy looks like and what its effects should be. I will offer guidance on how leaders can develop courageous advocacy wisely and attempt to demonstrate that not all issues of injustice are right for schools to address.

Importantly, I will explain the law as it stands and look at some exceptions for schools with a religious character. I will then demonstrate that a school can robustly pursue courageous advocacy without risking accusations of unlawful behaviour. My aim is to try to help leaders and governors to understand how their school's courageous advocacy can be soundly built on mainstream Christian theology, and how these theological roots can feed into a school's Christian vision. Demonstrating how curriculum and subject leaders can begin to embed the school's vision and courageous advocacy into their broader curriculum, I will show how courageous advocacy as part of a clearly stated theologically-rooted Christian vision can help schools to be accountable to their community and their parents, as well as to SIAMS and Ofsted.

My own vision for this book, then, is that it will help school leaders and governors to see courageous advocacy and its place at the heart of a school's Christian vision not as a burden for them to bear, but as a joyful expression of why they choose to give so much to their schools. I want them to be liberated so that they do not worry about breaking political impartiality rules or upsetting some members of the local community, but instead become confident to navigate through these potentially dangerous rapids without hitting any rocks. And most of all, I want to help them support the voters and leaders and activists of tomorrow to become confident and wise enough to bring about greater justice for the poor and the marginalized, whilst reducing the combative and polarized nature of so much of today's political discourse.

2 The Theology of Courageous Advocacy

In its 2001 report *The Way Ahead*, the Archbishops' Council states:

> The church school offers a spiritual and moral basis for the development of human wholeness and a sure foundation for personal and social values based on the person and ministry of Christ.[4]

In the light of this, the motivation for engaging a church school in courageous advocacy is not just moral but also spiritual and theological. Church school leaders may worry that, by explicitly referencing a theological rather than just a moral basis for courageous advocacy, they are undermining their duty to be inclusive. But *The Way Ahead*, even though it was written many years ago, still offers some of the best guidance to help church school leaders and governors navigate this dilemma.

The church school can provide all pupils, regardless of their family's professed faith, with courageous advocacy opportunities based on the example of Christ's ministry in the gospels, without threatening that family's beliefs or faith. Church school leaders need not be sheepish about this—to encourage pupils to be inspired by Christ's compassion or self-sacrifice is not to attempt to persuade them to become his disciples.

The SIAMS Inspection Framework helps schools with this by requiring that their leaders be able to articulate how their Christian vision is rooted in explicitly Christian theology. If a school's courageous advocacy very obviously arises from its Christian vision, then this theological framework is already in place.

The Person of Christ

It is subtly different to say that a Christian vision and associated courageous advocacy should be based on the person and ministry of Christ, rather than the beliefs of Christians. The gospels describe many different things that Christ did and said during his ministry. For a school's courageous advocacy to have maximum impact, they should not identify a cause and then root around in the gospels to find a convenient justification for doing it. Instead, they should start with their knowledge of their school's context and its Christian vision to decide what kind of courageous advocacy will most effectively support its principles that would have been reflected in any Church of England school's trust deed. While some schools have formally adopted this ethos statement, it can be equally useful to all Church of England schools attempting to operate in keeping with their trust deed, whether or not they can lay their hands on it.

The statement says:

> Recognizing its historic foundation, the school will preserve and develop its religious character in accordance with the principles of the church at parish and diocesan level.
>
> The school aims to serve its community by providing education of the highest quality within the context of Christian belief and practice. It encourages an understanding of the meaning and significance of faith and promotes Christian values through the experience it offers all its pupils.

The concept of courageous advocacy is a recent expression of this oldest and most fundamental requirement of a Church of England school—to provide education in the context of Christian belief and practice and to promote Christian values. For this reason, courageous advocacy is not something that some church schools may, or may not, choose, but is an essential way in which they fulfil their duty to live out their vision, educating pupils in keeping with their foundation.

4 Courageous Advocacy and Political Impartiality

In 2022 a primary school in Nottingham hit the headlines for encouraging some of its pupils to write to the prime minister accusing him of hypocrisy and calling for his resignation. In response to this, the Department for Education (DfE) published its *Political Impartiality in Schools* guidelines.[9] These guidelines did not include any new statutory requirements but reminded schools of their existing duties in law. Some school leaders and governors became worried that activities in their schools developing courageous advocacy among their pupils may have fallen foul of these guidelines, while other schools became worried about engaging in courageous advocacy at all.

Courageous advocacy in schools need not fall foul of these guidelines. In fact, by following these guidelines, schools will find that their courageous advocacy activities are the more effective, since they are less likely to involve empty words and more likely to engage in transformative action.

A school's two main legal duties related to political impartiality are set out in the Education Act 1996. The Act states that schools:

- must prohibit the promotion of partisan political views
- should take steps to ensure the balanced presentation of opposing views on political issues when they are brought to the attention of pupils.

Leaders and governors would be well advised to read the February 2022 guidelines for themselves, but there are some key points to consider. First is the DfE's definition of partisan political views. The guidelines state:

> Schools should be aware that 'partisan political views' are not limited to just political parties. They may also be held by campaign groups, lobbyists and charitable organisations.[10]

While all school leaders are aware that they should not promote any political party above another, they may well not have considered the role of campaign groups or charities in their schools. We have already looked, for example, at the key involvement of the charity Christian Aid in the development of the idea of courageous advocacy in schools. Does this mean that schools should not work with charities at all when it comes to courageous advocacy?

To answer this question, the guidelines helpfully distinguish between political issues and shared principles. Political issues are the key questions of the day, where political parties and other organizations disagree on the answers. The Department for Education guidelines do not define what such a political issue is, but they do say:

> some issues are clearly political, such as those relating to ongoing government activity or on which the main political parties have different views.[11]

These will change over time, but will usually include some perennial questions such as: public *versus* private delivery of services, immigration, the level and distribution of the tax burden and public spending on the military and overseas aid. Although there may well be a place for looking at these issues in a school's curriculum, the guidelines require that there should be a balanced presentation of opposing views. So if school leaders choose to encourage students to pursue courageous advocacy related to these political issues, they must take seriously the point of view that opposes what they are doing. To encourage students to do what is right whilst reminding them that they might be wrong is not impossible but may run the risk of undermining enthusiasm for the whole venture.

A school would be better advised to build its courageous advocacy on shared principles instead. The DofE guidelines say:

> Not all areas of ethical debate are political issues. There are some concepts and views that can be considered as shared principles that underpin our society and not political issues in this context. Examples include a belief in upholding certain rights, such as freedom of speech and protection from violence and criminal activity—or challenging discrimination and prejudice, including racism.[12]

This distinction between political issues and shared principles is very useful for schools and their courageous advocacy activities. If a school focuses on shared principles rather than political issues then the pitfalls are fewer and easier to avoid.

In planning courageous advocacy in school, leaders and governors may wish to ask themselves the following five questions:

> 1 Do mainstream parliamentary political parties disagree about it?

2 Is contested legislation passing through parliament now, or has it done so recently?

3 Even if political parties agree, is there a wider consensus in public opinion or continued debate, where different legitimate views are expressed?

4 Is it inconsistent with British values?

5 Does it go against the tenets of faith of the Church of England (or other denomination in a school with a religious character)?

If the answer to any of these questions is 'yes,' a school would be well advised to seek a different direction for their courageous advocacy.

Let us look at each question in turn.

Do mainstream parliamentary political parties disagree about it?
Any issue where there is significant disagreement between the government of the day and the main opposition parties in the House of Commons is, by definition, a political issue. While there may be unanimity about the nature of a problem, there may be disagreement on how best to solve it. An example of this could be the lack of affordable housing throughout the UK. Everyone agrees it is a problem, but political parties disagree on how to solve it. For a school to encourage pupils to lobby policymakers to build more social rather than private housing, or expand greenfield development, would be to fall into every trap that we have so far identified. This is because it could both cause division and encourage self-righteousness, while transforming no identifiable person's life for the better.

That is not to say that a school's courageous advocacy should not address the issue of homelessness. Instead, it should be done according to the Christian principle that it is our job to improve our neighbour's life rather than to tell a politician to do it for us, in keeping with the example of Jesus in the gospels. A school may well have a local charity that supports homeless people. Students could legitimately be encouraged to support this charity and to learn from it about the reasons why homelessness exists. They could then think about ways of addressing its causes and take action to help local homeless people. This can all be done without apportioning blame to a political party, potentially bringing about transformation for at least some homeless people, rather than drawing students into a political argument that transforms nobody. It is, after all, a Christian principle that it is our selfless actions which shame the powerful to act, rather than just our words, and it is those actions that give us the right to speak out.

Is contested legislation passing through parliament now, or has it done so recently?
This follows on from the first question but contains its own particular pitfalls. It is at the moment when a parliamentary bill becomes law that emotions can run highest, and we can make the mistake of treating a political issue as if it were a shared principle. In June 2020, during the first pandemic lockdown in the UK, the well-known footballer Marcus Rashford lobbied the government to reverse its decision to end an additional benefit to compensate some families for missing out on free school meals. His campaign was successful, winning him universal and deserved praise for his compassion and political acumen. He is rightly upheld in some schools as a good example of a courageous advocate, but it is important for schools to communicate to students that it is his *actions*, resulting from his opinions, which are being applauded. He stood up for what he believed to be right, as should we, but that does not mean that we have to agree with his beliefs.

Even if political parties agree, is there wider consensus in public opinion or continued debate, where different legitimate views are expressed?
This question requires even deeper wisdom from school leaders. There are some issues where a parliamentary consensus of opinion does not necessarily reflect unanimity in the nation as a whole. These issues can change over time and often vary in importance from school to school depending on its social context. Schools should rightly promote the rule of law, but it is not necessarily wise to dismiss the sensitivities of a school community simply because an issue of concern is allowed by law. Some communities, for example, have instincts that are more socially conservative than the tone of some legislation, especially if those communities include certain immigrant groups. The wise and compassionate school leader will take this into account when making decisions about courageous advocacy.

Is it consistent with British values?
All schools have a duty to 'actively promote' fundamental British values as set out by the government in the 2011 'Prevent' strategy.[13] These values are democracy, the rule of law, individual liberty, and mutual respect and tolerance of those with different faiths and beliefs.

While there is no compulsion for a school to use its courageous advocacy work to meet this requirement (as long as they are meeting it by other means), it is useful for school leaders to be able to explain their courageous advocacy in terms of these values, and at the very least to be sure that they do not contradict them. In particular, if students wish to support demonstrations over a particular issue of justice, the school should not encourage such action unless it is entirely lawful. In 2018, for example, the environmental activist Greta Thunberg launched a campaign of school strikes to demonstrate against climate change. While schools may rightly applaud her many lawful actions in favour of this shared principle, they should be careful not to promote this particular aspect of her activism. This is not to say that breaking the law in the name of a higher principle is always wrong, but rather to make the point that for a school to encourage a student to do it would be to act unlawfully.

Does it go against the tenets of faith of the Church of England (or other denomination in a school with a religious character)?
We have considered the theology of courageous advocacy in chapter two. All schools with a religious character have a trust deed which explains the denominational foundation of the school. Leaders and governors have a duty to run the school in keeping with this deed, by providing pupils with an education that is consistent with the principles of the denomination. It is very unlikely that a school would encourage its pupils to behave in a way that opposed accepted religious principles of peace, love and compassion, but leaders may nevertheless unwittingly imply that they approve of organizations that do. They should, therefore, take great care to avoid this.

Courageous Advocacy at the Heart of the Curriculum

5

Paragraph 2.2 of the National Curriculum in England states that:

> The school curriculum comprises all learning and other experiences that each school plans for its pupils. The national curriculum forms one part of the school curriculum.[14]

In paragraph 2.5 it goes on to say:

> Schools are also free to include other subjects or topics of their choice in planning and designing their own programme of education.

Courageous advocacy should, therefore, be treated as part of this programme of education. Just like any other curriculum subject, a school should have a clear intent about why they are encouraging a particular courageous advocacy theme and, very importantly, what they want pupils to know about it. Sometimes courageous advocacy can be packaged as part of character education. While it is true that it should contribute to the spiritual, moral, social and cultural development of pupils (referred to in the DfE's Character Education Framework Guidance, as well as Section 48 of the Education Act 2005, under which schools with a religious character are inspected), it should also contribute to what pupils know and remember.[15] And, as with any other subject, school leaders should be explicit about what they want this knowledge to be.

If, for example, a school wants its students to learn about, and take action to reverse, climate change, then it should be clear about what it wants its pupils to have learned about climate change because of their courageous advocacy topic. Similarly, if a school chooses anti-racism as a focus for courageous advocacy, what do they intend to teach their students about racism? Sometimes schools just assume this is obvious and press on with activities as if a consensus of knowledge and opinion existed. Yet this is unlikely to be the case. The opinions that one student hears in their home, or online, about climate change or racism will be very different from that of another. Before beginning such a responsible task with students, schools should distinguish fact from opinion and present those facts to pupils as part of the curriculum just as they would with anything else.

That does not mean that different opinions cannot be shared too, but schools should distinguish between fact and opinion. With anti-racism, for example, facts can be taught about the history of the global slave trade, alongside the experiences of prejudice recalled by victims of racism in the UK and in other countries. The different analysis of the problem, and recommendations for action arising from this analysis, can also be taught, but with the proviso that this is opinion rather than fact. In an age-appropriate way, for example, students could consider the conclusions of the 2023 Casey Report, or the TUC's 2022 'Racism in the UK Labour Market' report, alongside the 2021 Sewell Report published by the Commission on Race and Ethnic Disparities.[16] In dealing with such a sensitive subject, schools should take at least as much care in preparing what will be taught as they would for any other part of the curriculum.

Whilst such knowledge is necessary for students to become effective agents for change, however, it is not sufficient. In the final chapter, we will look at the necessity of turning knowledge into action which transforms the lives of identifiable people for the better for something truly to be called courageous advocacy.

An additional challenge is that schools with a religious character must also take their foundation's denominational beliefs into account when planning courageous advocacy in the curriculum. The government's guidelines on political impartiality in schools state:

> Schools designated with a religious character are free to teach according to the tenets of their faith. We do not consider principles or views in line with these tenets to be covered by statutory requirements on political impartiality.[17]

The guidance offers no further advice but there are certain issues, which some people view as examples of injustice, which are not seen as such by the foundation faiths of some of our schools. These might include abortion and birth control, sexual identity or the definition of holy matrimony. Wise leaders and governors may well conclude that these issues are best covered in the school's relationships and sex education (RSE) curriculum, where they can be considered thoughtfully and difference of opinion can be acknowledged, rather than as a courageous advocacy activity, where there may well be disagreement about the nature of the truth which needs to be spoken to power. Paragraph 21 of the DfE's statutory RSE guidance states:

> Schools with a religious character may teach the distinctive faith perspective on relationships, and balanced debate may take place about issues that are seen as contentious.[18]

It is possible that school leaders might be approached by a group of students, parents or governors suggesting a courageous advocacy focus that promotes a particular position on such an issue. If that happens, leaders should be prepared to explain that these issues are instead addressed in the RSE curriculum.

A more difficult issue could be if a courageous advocacy idea is suggested where the issue of justice has religion at its heart. In 2018 a group of schoolgirls were abducted from their school in Nigeria by an extremist Islamicist group. Shortly afterwards, all the girls were released except one, named Leah Sharibu. Unlike the others, she refused to agree to convert to Islam in return for her freedom. Her case has been taken up by the UK registered charity Christian Solidarity Worldwide (CSW) under the title #freeleah. On their website, CSW provide helpful information about how supporters can campaign for her release by, among other things, writing to the Nigerian High Commissioner in London asking for more urgent action to be taken.

Some leaders of a school with a religious character and a Christian denominational foundation might consider this to be an admirable focus for courageous advocacy. A Church of England school, for example, might think that this perfectly reflects the Anglican principles which their foundation requires them to have at the heart of their curriculum. While nobody could fail to feel sympathy and respect for Leah, and nobody could disagree with CSW's vision for a world free from religious persecution, there may be reasons why her case should not be chosen as a courageous advocacy focus, even though the school may remember this admirable young woman in their prayers during their daily act of collective worship. The step-by-step guide provided in the next chapter may help to clarify this.

Another dilemma faced by a school with a religious character is how they react to public statements about political policy made by the leaders of their foundation religion. In his 2022 Easter sermon, the Archbishop of Canterbury, Justin Welby, described a government plan to send some asylum seekers from the UK to Rwanda as 'the opposite of the nature of God.' He went on to say that there were 'serious ethical questions about sending asylum seekers overseas,' and that the 'principle must stand the judgment of God, and it cannot.'[19]

On the one hand, here is a political issue that should be treated with great caution as a topic for courageous advocacy. On the other hand, we have seen that the statutory requirements on political impartiality do not apply to a Church of England school on matters that are included in the tenets of their faith. An Anglican school could then argue that, by definition, a statement from the Archbishop of Canterbury must be part of the tenets of the faith of the Church of England, so they are free to encourage students to campaign against the injustice of the Rwanda policy.

While this opinion may technically have some merit, it is built on weak foundations. Does every utterance of the Archbishop of Canterbury immediately become a tenet of the Church of England? Probably not. Also, does the fact that the archbishop has a particular view mean that there will now be unanimity within the school community that his view is the right one? Almost certainly not.

In the press there was much criticism of Archbishop Justin for these comments, with many commentators advising him to stick to churchmanship and avoid politics. Yet in saying this, many writers betrayed their own ignorance of the British constitutional establishment. As well as being church leaders, a few Church of England bishops have the right to sit in the House of Lords as lords spiritual. This ancient right, enshrined in the Church of England as the established church, means that, for some of the time, these archbishops and bishops are also politicians. As such, it is not just their right but is also their duty to speak out on political matters. A lord spiritual should no more keep their nose out of politics than should an elected member of parliament—but comments made by church leaders in the House of Lords should not be taken as a reflection of the views of the church, but rather the expression of the conscience of the individual bishop. Therefore such comments cannot give schools a green light to reflect that opinion as the morally right option in a politically contested debate, and schools should not be tempted to do this.

Courageous Advocacy—Making the Wise Choice

6

Before putting together our step-by-step guide to developing successful courageous advocacy in school, we should ask ourselves what it is that makes advocacy into something truly courageous. In his introduction to the Church of England/Christian Aid 'Courageous Advocacy' document, Derek Holloway describes the best examples of courageous advocacy as looking 'beyond the local, the current and the fashionable to the global, the long-term and the unfashionable.'

In describing effective courageous advocacy in this way, Holloway is highlighting its essential prophetic nature. An important characteristic of biblical prophets is that, when speaking out what they believed to be the word of God, they always made themselves unpopular with the powers that be. Elijah fled the wrath of Jezebel, Jeremiah was cast into a cistern, whilst John the Baptist was beheaded. Prophets require courage, especially when they are following Holloway's advice to be unfashionable.

The most important duty that school leaders have, though, is to keep their pupils safe

The most important duty that school leaders have, though, is to keep their pupils safe. In this context, that might mean *not* drawing them into arguments where emotions run high and where they might become the focus of someone's criticism or unkindness. Schools are right to protect their children from danger by not expecting them to be courageous enough to attract criticism, acknowledging that this may sometimes take the courage out of courageous advocacy. Unfashionable does not have to be controversial—it might just be a bit boring.

One area where it is particularly important to keep pupils safe is when a school considers its attitude to war and military conflict. English schools are becoming increasingly multiethnic. Government data shows that the proportion of pupils in English schools from a minority ethnic background was 35.7% for the academic year 2022/23, up from 33.2% in 2019/20.[20] The proportion of pupils whose first language is not English is 20.2%. In nurseries, the figure is 30.4%. The direction of travel for schools will, therefore, continue to be upwards for a number of years to come.

Most military conflicts are complicated, and schools are wise not to be seen to take sides when planning courageous advocacy in the curriculum. The civil war in Syria is a case in point. Many schools are likely to contain refugee families who have suffered at the hands of all the different military groups involved in the conflict, so to express sympathy with one group against another would be cruel and schools should be careful not to do this.

It is more difficult when a conflict is religious as well as ethnic. Church schools, for example, should be careful of taking the 'Christian' side in an armed conflict, as this is to imply that warfare in the name of Christ is a legitimate expression of the Christian faith. Some church schools, particularly in London, have a significant Nigerian population. Nigeria suffers from an ongoing ethnic conflict where the two opposing groups often characterize themselves as Christian and Muslim. A school's Nigerian families will inevitably include Muslims as well as Christians, so school leaders should think deeply before expressing any support for the 'Christian' side, even though the school may have a Christian denominational foundation.

At the time of writing, Ukraine is fighting off a Russian military invasion. England has welcomed many Ukrainian refugees from the conflict and many schools, including church schools, display the Ukrainian flag to show their support. This is understandable—after all, it clearly must be a shared principle that a nation state should not be invaded by its neighbour. Many schools are rightly welcoming Ukrainian families into their communities and offering them high levels of support. However, some schools also have Russian families, who may well have relatives in Russia who support, or even serve in, the Russian military, and whose feelings about the war may be mixed. If support for Ukraine in a school goes beyond a sense of compassion for all, to become an aspect of courageous advocacy in the curriculum, leaders would be wise to reflect on what issues of justice related to Ukraine are taught in the curriculum, alongside what—and to whom—pupils may be encouraged to say to those in power whose decisions may prolong or curtail the war.

In this booklet I have invited the reader to consider the many aspects of the concept of courageous advocacy which school leaders should take into account when promoting it as part of their school's curriculum. I finish by offering a list of questions against which they can check whether a courageous advocacy idea is right for their school. It is not scientific and leaders should give more weighting to some questions than others to reflect their school's context. To answer 'yes' to a question is to imply a green light, whilst a 'no' implies amber or even red. I hope leaders find it useful.

Courageous Advocacy Checklist

Did pupils contribute to choosing the idea?
Guidance from teachers is always helpful, but pupils must care about an issue of justice if they are to embrace and act upon it. Leaders should make it easy for pupils to come to them with suggestions.

Is it based on a shared principle rather than a political issue?
This is explained in chapter four.

Is it consistent with British values?
Are the values of democracy, the rule of law, individual liberty and tolerance of difference at the heart of the activity? Adults may well apply some civil disobedience to make their voice heard, but a school should never encourage its students to break the law.

Does it reflect the school's (Christian) vision?
If pupils are motivated to take action in a way that cannot be easily explained in terms of a school's vision, maybe the school needs a new vision.

Can it easily be embraced by the school community?
If a proposed act of courageous advocacy makes a significant proportion of the school community uncomfortable, it might be wiser to start by gently changing hearts and minds rather than openly promoting action.

In a school with a religious character, is it a reflection of the theology of the foundation denomination?
If there is no obvious connection between these two things, leaders may seek to consult with their foundation governors for clarification.

Is it global, long-term and unfashionable?
Global is not automatically better than local, but addressing only local issues can encourage parochialism. Long-term impact is best—litter-picking is a laudable thing to do, but will the litter be back next week? There is nothing inherently wrong with choosing a fashionable cause, but to do something only because it is fashionable is likely to feel tokenistic.

Do pupils have to be courageous?
Children should never be put in danger, but how can they be brave? This could involve public speaking, or meeting with adult decision-makers whom children perceive to be intimidating. To be memorable and effective, courageous advocacy should push everyone a little way out of their comfort zone.

Does it involve action rather than just expressing opinions?
Demands for those in power to act should be matched by action from pupils too. Without this, courageous advocacy can descend into self-righteousness.

Does it transform identifiable people's lives for the better?
If the beneficiaries cannot be identified and the benefit explained, then it is activism rather than advocacy. If a globally significant example of injustice, such as climate change or racism, is to be addressed, a school should still identify an individual or group of individuals whose lives are made better. For climate change, an international charity might, for example, help a school to identify a community stricken by drought, where a school could help to provide a water pump, whilst also campaigning at a national or international level for legislative change. As for racism, schools should avoid the self-righteousness of trying to make certain groups less racist. Instead, they might encourage a greater social connection between different racial groups, either within a school or between schools. This has the advantage of avoiding the implication that one racial group is somehow more racist than another, as this is not a judgment that a school would wisely wish to make.

Is it embedded in the curriculum in more than a token way?
A standalone lesson about Rosa Parks does not embed anti-racist courageous advocacy into a school's curriculum. What body of knowledge will form the intent? How will it be implemented? And how will the school assess its impact?

I recently visited a Church of England school in London. My taxi driver refused to drop me off outside the gates, instead insisting on dropping me around the corner. When I recounted this to the headteacher, she explained that her pupils were to blame. Until recently, many parents had been ignoring waiting restrictions for vehicles outside the school entrance at the beginning and end of the school day. Because of this, older pupils felt in danger, and were particularly concerned about the safety of younger children and their parents being forced to walk around the illegally parked cars. Supported by staff, the pupils invited local councillors to visit the school and asked for parking cameras to be installed. The council complied, and the problem was solved.

This example of courageous advocacy scored highly on the above checklist. Even though it was local, I know that the school balances this with courageous advocacy in the curriculum that looks at global issues too.

If you are a school leader or teacher looking for guidance about how to develop courageous advocacy in your school, I hope this booklet has empowered you to seek out ideas that will support your pupils and students to become the agents for change that our society so desperately needs, both now and in the future.

Notes

1 Ofsted, *School Inspection Handbook* (2022), paragraph 211: https://www.gov.uk/government/publications/school-inspection-handbook-eif/school-inspection-handbook

2 C Weir, *Courageous Advocacy* (Church of England Education Office and Christian Aid, 2021) https://www.churchofengland.org/sites/default/files/2021-05/180521%20Courageous%20Advocacy%20%28final%29.pdf

3 G Orwell, *All Art is Propaganda: Critical Essays* (Sahara Publisher Books, 1940.)

4 Archbishops' Council, *The Way Ahead: Church of England Schools in the New Millennium* (London: Church House Publishing, 2000).

5 Church of England Education Office, 'SIAMS—An Evaluation Schedule for Schools and Inspectors 2018 Updated September 2022': FINAL—SIAMS Evaluation Schedule (revised July 2022).pdf (churchofengland.org).

6 Church of England Education Office, 'SIAMS Framework September 2023': SIAMS Framework September 2023.pdf (churchofengland.org).

7 Church of England Education Office, 'Church of England Vision for Education—Deeply Christian, Serving the Common Good' (2016): Layout 1 (churchofengland.org).

8 Church of England Education Office, 'SIAMS Methodist Principles for Education' (2022): SIAMS Methodist Principles of Education 220714.pdf (churchofengland.org).

9 Department for Education, 'Political Impartiality in Schools' (2022): Political impartiality in schools—GOV.UK (www.gov.uk)..

10 *ibid.*

11 *ibid.*

12 *ibid.*

13 H M Government, 'Prevent Strategy' (2011): Prevent review (publishing.service.gov.uk).

14 Department for Education, 'The National Curriculum in England' (2014): National curriculum—GOV.UK (www.gov.uk).

15 Department for Education, 'Character Education Framework Guidance' (2019): Character education framework—GOV.UK (www.gov.uk).

16 See Baroness Casey, 'Review into the standards of behaviour and internal culture of the Metropolitan Police Service' (2023); TUC, 'Still Rigged: racism in the UK labour market' (2022); T Sewell, 'The Report of the Commission on Race and Ethnic Disparities' (2021).

17 Department for Education 2022, *op cit.*

18 Department for Education, 'Relationships Education, Relationships and Sex Education (RSE) and Health Education' (2019): Relationships and sex education (RSE) and health education—GOV.UK (www.gov.uk)

19 The Archbishop of Canterbury, Archbishop's Easter sermon at Canterbury Cathedral Sung Eucharist.

20 Department for Education, 'Schools, pupils and their characteristics' (2023): https://explore-education-statistics.service.gov.uk/find-statistics/school-pupils-and-their-characteristics